THANK ME LATER

Real Estate
Career and Financial Freedom Blueprint

How I made 40 Multi-Millionaires?

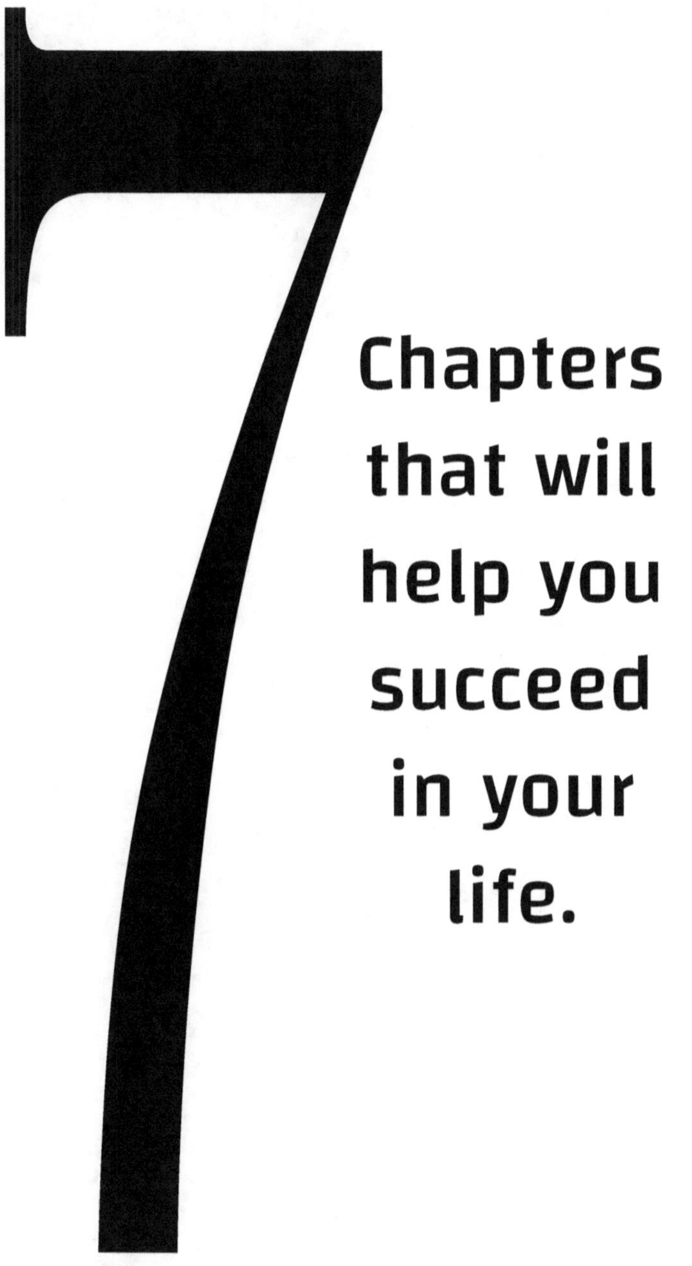

Chapters that will help you succeed in your life.

THANK ME LATER

Real Estate
Career and Financial Freedom Blueprint

SACHIN ARORA

Worldwide Published by
Pendown Press

PENDOWN PRESS
An ISO 9001 & ISO 14001 Certified Co.,
Regd. Office: 2525/193, 1st Floor, Onkar Nagar-A,
Tri Nagar, Delhi-110035
Ph.: 09350849407, 09312235086
E-mail: info@pendownpress.com
Branch Office: 1A/2A, 20, Hari Sadan, Ansari Road,
Daryaganj, New Delhi-110002
Ph.: 011-45794768
Website: PendownPress.com

First Edition: 2023

ISBN: 978-93-5554-497-1

Layout and Cover Designed by Pendown Graphics Team
Printed and Bound in India by Thomson Press India Ltd.

Contents

"People may sometimes resent my tough expectations for the team as it challenges them to stay focused. But I always reassure them with my catchphrase, "Thank me later," emphasizing that the effort put in today will pay off in the future."

~Sachin Arora

Foreword

It is my pleasure to write the foreword for Sachin Arora's book "**Thank Me Later.**" Sachin has been a leading figure in the real estate industry for many years and has a wealth of knowledge and experience to share with aspiring real estate sales professionals.

In this book, Sachin lays out a comprehensive guide to starting a successful real estate sales career. He covers everything from the basics of real estate sales to the more advanced strategies for success. With his clear and concise writing style, Sachin makes it easy for readers to understand and follow the steps to success in this exciting and lucrative field.

Whether you are just starting out in your real estate sales career or are looking to take your skills to the next level, this book is an essential resource. I highly recommend it to anyone who is passionate about real estate and is looking to build a successful career in this industry.

Sachin has a true talent for communicating complex ideas in a simple and accessible way, and this book is a testament to that. I am confident that "**Thank Me Later**" will be an invaluable resource for anyone looking to start or advance their real estate sales career.

~Diwakur Singh

Executive Director

Chandigarh University

(Online and Distance Learning)

Preface

As the real estate industry continues to evolve and grow, there has never been a better time to start a career in real estate sales. Whether you are just starting out or looking to make a career change, real estate sales offers a wealth of opportunities for those who are willing to work hard and learn the ropes.

In this book, I have distilled my years of experience and expertise in the real estate industry into a comprehensive guide for aspiring real estate sales professionals. I cover everything from the basics of real estate sales to the more advanced strategies for success, providing readers with a step-by-step blueprint for building a successful real estate sales career.

This book is not just for those who are new to real estate sales but for those who are looking to take their skills to the next level. Whether you are an experienced real estate sales professional or just starting out, this book is packed with valuable insights and practical advice to help you succeed in this exciting and rewarding field.

I wrote this book with the goal of empowering aspiring real estate sales professionals with the knowledge and tools they need to build a successful career. I believe that with the right guidance and a strong work ethic, anyone can achieve success in the real estate industry

I hope that this book will inspire and empower you to pursue your real estate sales career with confidence and to take your skills to new heights. I wish you all the best in your journey and look forward to seeing your success in the world of real estate sales.

Introduction: Some Vital Questions that Need Answers

Are you considering a career in real estate sales but feeling uncertain about how to get started? If so, you're not alone. Many people are attracted to the idea of working in the real estate industry but don't know from where to begin.

Let me ask you something: Are you a freelancer agent or an entrepreneur in the real estate industry?

There's a big difference between being a freelancer agent and an entrepreneur in the real estate industry, and many people don't realize this distinction, leading them down the wrong path.

I have helped hundreds of people become real estate entrepreneurs under my umbrella, and I'm willing to help more people.

I understand you may have questions like:

- "How can I build a stable and secure real estate sales career?"

- "How can I confidently break into the industry without fear of failure?"
- "How can I supplement my retirement income with real estate sales?"
- "How can I ensure I won't waste time and resources on something I won't like or that won't generate the income I want?"
- "How can I finally figure out which direction to take? I feel so lost."

The abundance of information about real estate sales can be overwhelming, but don't let it discourage you from reaching your goals. I'm here to guide you through the steps you need to take before you start your search.

You don't want to waste your resources on something that doesn't make you happy or bring in enough income.

It's time to finally make a definitive decision and take control of your real estate sales career.

I have a step-by-step framework to help you become a successful real estate sales professional, and I want to show you just how easy it is to get started.

More security, more income, and more freedom are all within your reach by building a monetizable skill set and trading those skills for money. Read this book thoroughly, and it'll help you create your very own freedom plan for a successful real estate sales career. You'll learn about all the opportunities in the real estate industry and how to choose a profitable path that's right for you.

I can't wait to see you succeed in your Real Estate Sales Career!

From Struggle to Success: My Growth Journey

I was born in the small town of Panipat, Haryana, India, with big dreams and a desire to see the world. While Growing up, I faced many challenges, but I never lost sight of my dreams. This book is the summarized version of my real estate sales success journey, from the early days of my career to the present, and the critical lessons I learned along the way.

My Early Career

I grew up in a close-knit middle-class family, surrounded by everyday challenges and happiness. My parents instilled in me a love of learning and a strong work ethic. I was always curious and eager to explore the world around me. However, the early stage of my real estate sales career was not without its challenges.

After my MBA was completed, I struggled in the first 24 months to see my first real money in hand. Throughout my career, I never considered pursuing a job in the government sector. I had always been motivated by the prospect of unlimited potential for growth and financial success, which I believed would be difficult to achieve within the limitations of a government position. That's why I turned my attention towards real estate, a field that offered me the opportunity to apply my skills and expertise in a way that aligned with my personal and professional goals.

I found real estate to be a perfect fit for me, as it allowed me to work towards achieving my financial aspirations and explore various creative avenues for personal and professional development.

The Key Moments and Decisions

Despite facing challenges, I never lost my love for learning and my ambition to achieve great success in the real estate sales market in Noida. I met my now-wife, Jyoti Kapoor, during my undergraduate studies while also preparing for the Chartered Accountancy Exam in Panipat. Seeking further education, I made the decision at the age of 21 to leave home and attend college in the city to earn my MBA. These were pivotal moments in my life as I finally had the chance to chase my aspirations and explore new possibilities.

The Turning Points

After earning my MBA, I went to several job interviews but found it difficult to secure a suitable position. When I was offered a job, the salary was lower than I expected, and I felt that it would not allow me to live the life I desired. In search of a path to financial success, I decided to enter the real estate sales industry in Noida. Here, *I would like to express my immense gratitude to my mentor, Mr. Deepak Chhabra (Corporate Director, Investors Clinic), for introducing me to The Investors Clinic. Additionally, I owe a great deal of my success to Mr. Honey Katiyal (Founder-CEO, Investors Clinic), under whose guidance and leadership I was able to flourish. Also, I am grateful to Mr. Amit Raheja who taught me a lot.* This proved to be a significant turning point in my career, but it also brought new obstacles, such as the need to perform well under pressure and work in a fast-paced environment. Despite the initial struggles, including not understanding the revenue model of the real estate market, I remained focused on my goals and worked hard to overcome these challenges.

Challenges: The Stepping Stones to Success

One of the biggest challenge I faced was achieving nothing despite spending the first 24 months in Real Estate Sales.

The situation became such that:

1. Balancing the responsibilities of family, friendships, and social events proved to be a formidable challenge.

2. I had to repeat the same piece of clothing due to financial constraints, but I was determined not to let my circumstance define my confidence and resilience.

3. As I was residing here without family, I had to limit myself to a single meal per day. Although I was going through a difficult financial situation, I remained optimistic and confident that I would overcome it.

4. Due to my demanding schedule, I struggled to allocate enough time to celebrate special personal and memorable moments with my now-wife & parents.

5. Despite feeling lonely and disorganized, I maintained a positive outlook and believed that I would overcome these challenges in due time.

Let me share two personal stories of challenges that triggered my determination to succeed.

a. Back when I was dating my now-wife Jyoti, I was like any other person in love, always yearning to spend more time with her. Even though she lived in Rohini, a good 50 kilometers away from my residence, I would travel for two to two-and-a-half hours using public transport by auto and metro just to see her for a mere 10 to 15 minutes. Despite the long and arduous journey, I remained optimistic that things would change for the better soon.

b. One day, I ordered a meal and attempted to pay for it using my SBI card. To my dismay, the payment did not go through, as my card had been blocked by SBI due to my inability to pay the minimum balance. This unfortunate situation only became worse as I began to receive collection calls on a regular basis. Frustrated and feeling helpless, I made a vow to myself to take control of my finances and never find myself in a similar situation again. The experience was a crushing blow that left me feeling angry and frustrated, but it also served as a wakeup call and inspired me to take action towards better financial management.

I emphasize my challenges not to brag about my achievements but to share what I have learned from all the adverse situations.

The Valuable Lessons Learned

Throughout my journey, I learned the importance of perseverance, friendship, and the power of following your dreams. I also learned that success is not just about achieving your goals but also about the relationships and experiences along the way.

Moreover, out of my learnings, I have designed my life based on four philosophies.

I. **Either the Best One or the Only One:** The guiding philosophy of my life centers on the pursuit of excellence, with the ultimate goal of achieving the top position in any endeavor I undertake. I firmly believe that this is the key to success and that the pursuit of greatness is a never-ending journey. I am not alone in this belief, as many successful people throughout history have emphasized the importance of striving to be the best in one's field. This philosophy requires dedication, hard work, and a willingness to learn and grow. It demands a constant effort to improve oneself, to stay ahead of the curve, and never settle for mediocrity.

II. **Strive for excellence, and money will follow:** When one is dedicated to excellence, they tend to stand out from their peers and are often sought after for their expertise. This can lead to more opportunities, greater job satisfaction and ultimately financial success. In essence, the pursuit of excellence is a virtuous cycle that can lead to long-term personal and professional fulfillment.

    Moreover, the pursuit of excellence is not limited to the workplace. It can apply to all aspects of life, including personal relationships, hobbies and other interests. By constantly striving to improve oneself and to reach one's full potential, one can live a more fulfilling and meaningful life.

    In conclusion, the belief that "striving for excellence, and money will follow" can be a powerful motivator for personal and professional success. However, **it's important to approach the pursuit of excellence with a sincere desire to improve and to do one's best rather than solely for the purpose of financial gain.**

III. **Celebrate every small success:** Celebrating every small success is an important practice I have developed that has a positive impact on our personal and professional lives. It involves acknowledging and taking pride in even the smallest accomplishments rather than just waiting for the big victories to celebrate.

By celebrating even small successes, we can boost our confidence and motivation and keep ourselves focused on achieving our goals. It can also help us appreciate the journey and the progress we are making rather than just the end result.

Moreover, celebrating small successes can be a source of inspiration and encouragement to others. When we share our successes, we can inspire and motivate others to pursue their own goals and celebrate their own small wins.

It's important to note that celebrating small successes doesn't have to be a grand affair. It can be as simple as taking a moment to reflect on what we've achieved, giving ourselves a pat on the back, or treating ourselves to something we enjoy. It's about taking the time to acknowledge and appreciate the effort and progress we've made.

In conclusion, celebrating every small success is a valuable practice that can have a positive impact on our personal and professional lives. It can help us to stay motivated, appreciate our progress, and inspire others to pursue their own goals. So, let's take the time to celebrate every small win and enjoy the journey of achieving our goals.

IV. **First Family vs Family First:** I strongly believe in the philosophy that **my team is my first family,** and **I see my colleagues as brothers and sisters of another mother.** I prioritize the success of the team and always try to support my colleagues in any way possible. While I understand the importance of family commitments, **I also know that being part of a strong and supportive team can help us achieve a better work-life balance and ultimately benefit our personal relationships as well.** That's why I always strive to contribute to the success of the team and create a positive and collaborative work culture where everyone feel valued and supported.

Living My Best Life by Design

Today, I am living my dream as a successful Real Estate Entrepreneur in Noida with a team of 200+ people. I have helped more than 40 people in my team become multi-millionaires. While many people often measure their net worth in terms of their physical assets, I personally consider my net worth to be the number of individuals I've had the privilege to work with over the years. Specifically, out of the 216 people I've had the pleasure of working alongside, 70 of them have been with me for 5 years, 35 for 8 years, and 8 for more than 10 years. These individuals have chosen to stay with me because of the care and support I have provided them, and I am grateful for the relationships I have formed with each of them. Today, my closest friends and brothers are individuals from diverse states, regions, languages, and cultures, to whom I met through walking interviews.

I have traveled to many amazing places and met incredible people, and I feel grateful for every experience. I have also found love and started a family, which has brought new joy and fulfillment to my life.

And the Journey Continues...

This book is an expression of my gratitude for the journey that has brought me to where I am today and to the people who want to build their careers in real estate sales. **It is a reminder to never give up on your dreams, to cherish the people in your life, and to live every day to the fullest.** I started my career as a sales executive, and I worked hard and dedicated myself to the job. I was committed to learning and growing, and it paid off when I was promoted to the position of director within the same company in just 7.5 years.

Starting as a sales executive was not easy, but I was determined to succeed. I knew it would take hard work and perseverance to advance in my career. I focused on delivering results, taking the initiative, and consistently going above and beyond my job requirements.

Becoming a director in the same company after just 7.5 years was a huge achievement for me. It showed that my hard work, dedication, and commitment to the company paid off. It was a true testament to my sustained high performance, unwavering dedication, and strong work ethic.

For me, one of the keys to success is setting clear goals and objectives and working hard to achieve them. It also means being open to learning, taking risks, and being adaptable in a changing environment.

Why am I Writing this Book?

Throughout my years in the real estate sales industry, I have seen countless individual's struggle to get their career off the ground or take them to the next level.

I know what it takes to be successful in this field, and I have a wealth of knowledge and experience to share.

That's why I wrote this book - to help others to avoid the common pitfalls and mistakes that can slow down their progress and to provide them with the tools and guidance they need to succeed.

Some people may worry that sharing the secrets of my success in this book will be perceived as a mistake, as it may lead others to copy my strategies and become my competitors.

However, **my main objective for writing this book is to give back to both, society and the real estate industry. By sharing my knowledge and experience, I hope to contribute to the growth and success of the industry as a whole and to help others achieve their own success.**

While there may be risks involved in sharing my secrets, I believe that the potential benefits far outweigh them. Ultimately, my goal is to make a positive impact and help others in any way I can.

I always yearned for financial freedom, and after exploring various career options, I found real estate sales to be the best fit for me. While many of my friends and relatives pursued higher education and landed jobs with impressive salaries, **I was and am convinced that the growth potential in the real estate sector is unmatched.**

Over time, my hard work and dedication to the field paid off, and I experienced fast-track growth in my career, which took many of my family and friends by surprise. They were amazed at the level of financial success I had achieved through real estate sales, and soon enough, many of them decided to join me.

It was gratifying to see those who had previously worked in IT jobs, FMCG jobs, and held prestigious titles like CA and CS embrace the real estate field and thrive in it, just as I had done.

I was proud and humbled at the same time to have made an impact in their lives by pursuing my own dream.

I believe that success in real estate sales requires a combination of technical knowledge, practical skills, and the right mindset.

This book covers everything from the basics of starting a real estate career to becoming up and running. Whether you're just starting out in your career or you're looking to take your skills to the next level, I'm confident that you'll find the information and insights in this book to be invaluable.

So if you're serious about building a successful career in real estate sales, then I invite you to go through this book thoroughly today and start your journey towards success.

Chapter 1

An Overview of The Real Estate Industry

Real Estate as an Industry

The real estate industry in India has seen significant growth in recent years, driven by factors such as urbanization and the growth of the country's middle class.

According to a report by the Confederation of Real Estate Developers' Associations of India (CREDAI), the Indian real estate market size was valued at around $180 billion in 2020 and is expected to reach $1 trillion by 2030.

The report also suggests that the industry's contribution to the country's gross domestic product (GDP) is expected to increase from 5-6% in 2020 to 13% by 2025.

The Indian government's "Housing for All" initiative and the introduction of the Real Estate Regulation and Development Act (RERA) in 2016 have also played a crucial role in the growth of the industry. The RERA has helped to bring transparency and accountability to the real estate sector and has boosted the confidence of buyers and investors in the industry.

The commercial and retail sectors are also growing at a steady pace, with an increase in office space and shopping mall developments across the country. E-commerce has also been a key driver of the growth of the retail sector.

The real estate industry provides employment opportunities not only directly but also indirectly through various allied industries such as cement, steel, construction and many more.

In addition, the growth of the real estate industry has a positive impact on the overall economic growth of the country by increasing investment and boosting consumer spending.

Real Estate as a Career Market

The real estate sector is considered to be the second-highest employment-generating sector in India, directly or indirectly

Here is a list of a few of the many career options real estate offers

- Real Estate Sales.
- Real Estate Marketing
- Real Estate Leasing/Renting
- Client Relationship Management (CRM)
- Property Valuation
- Legal & Compliances
- Property Management

Out of the list above, I will be talking about the extremely promising Real Estate Sales as a career in this book.

One of the main benefits of a career in real estate sales in India is the potential for high earnings as the market has been continuously growing.

The rising demand for housing, especially in the affordable housing segment, and the increasing investment in commercial and retail spaces have created many opportunities for professionals in the industry.

However, it is important to note that earnings can vary greatly based on factors such as experience, the local real estate market, and sales volume.

A major challenge in the Indian market is that the industry also has a reputation for lack of transparency and trust, which can make it difficult for agents or salespersons to establish themselves and build a client base.

Besides the challenges, the exciting fact is:

"According to NAR-India, 80% of real estate transactions in India happen through Real Estate Consultants, Agents, Brokers, or Salespersons only."

Why is Sales a Better Career Option?

Sales is a challenging but rewarding career that can provide numerous benefits to individuals who are motivated, goal-oriented, and have strong communication and interpersonal skills.

Here are some additional benefits of a career in sales:

- **Independence:** Many sales roles allow individuals to work independently, giving them the freedom to manage their own schedules and work styles.
- **Customer interaction:** Sales professionals have the opportunity to interact with customers and build relationships, which can be fulfilling and provide a sense of purpose.

- **Opportunities for travel:** Sales roles that involve traveling can provide individuals with the chance to visit new places and broaden their perspectives.
- **Challenging and dynamic:** Sales is a constantly evolving field that requires individuals to adapt to new products, markets, and technologies. This can keep work interesting and challenging.
- **Unlimited earning potential:** Sales professionals who consistently meet or exceed their targets can earn unlimited commissions and bonuses, which can lead to significant earnings.

"It is always said that sales is the only profession where a salesperson can write their own pay-cheque every month, and Real Estate Sales is Tendulkar here."

Chapter 2

Real Estate Sales as a Career Option

I feel fortunate that I got into real estate sales, and I achieved everything beyond what I could have imagined as a middle-class boy at the earliest stage of my life.

I always dreamt of giving a comfortable life to my family and kids. I always wanted that money should not come in between and be the limitation while taking important decisions for my family and me, be it good clothes, healthy food, travelling abroad, owning a comfortable luxury home, dream car, better education, quality medical support and charity.

These were the driving forces at the beginning of my career, and I have achieved them all.

During my work, apart from the above reasons, I found the following prominent reasons which kept me attracted towards a real estate sales career.

- **High earning potential:** Real estate sales has the potential to earn a high income, especially if you are successful in building a relationship and serving a large client base and consistently closing deals.
- **Independence:** A career in real estate sales allows for a high degree of autonomy and flexibility. People are able to set their own schedule and work independently rather than being tied to a traditional 9-to-5 work schedule.
- **Personal fulfillment:** Many people find that a career in real estate sales is personally fulfilling, as they are able to help people buy the most important asset in their life, their home.
- **Potential for growth:** Real estate is an industry that has a huge potential for growth. The rise in the economy and the rise in population growth are increasing the demand for housing and commercial spaces. A career in real estate sales can be an excellent way to take advantage of this growing market.
- **Constant learning:** Real estate is an ever-changing industry, with new laws, regulations, and market trends constantly evolving. Salespeople are expected to stay informed and educated about these changes, providing opportunities for learning and professional development.

- **Networking opportunities:** A career in real estate sales provides ample opportunities to meet and network with a wide variety of people, from clients to other industry professionals.

Sales vs Real Estate Sales: Difference

In addition to the factors mentioned above, there are other important factors that make real estate sales distinct from other sales profiles.

1. **Personalized sales vs Channelized sales:**

   Real estate sales typically involve personalized sales, where the focus is on building relationships with clients and providing tailored solutions to meet their unique needs. In contrast, other sales profiles, such as retail or online sales, often involve channelized sales, where the focus is on showcasing a range of products to a wider audience.

2. **Unique features of properties:**

   In Real Estate Sales, each property has unique features that must be learned and understood separately by agents. This is in contrast to Other Sales Profiles, where products typically have standardized features and benefits.

3. **Work location:**

   Real Estate Sales is not a work-from-home job, as agents need to be out in the field to show properties, meet with clients, and attend networking events. Other Sales Profiles, such as telesales or online sales, can often be done remotely.

4. **Emotional process:**

   Real Estate Sales is an emotional process, as it often involves a significant and emotional purchase, such as buying a first home. In contrast, Other Sales Profiles may involve less emotional purchases, such as buying a pair of shoes.

5. **Extensive research and planning:**

   Real estate sales require extensive research and planning, with buyers often spending more time on this purchase than any other. Multiple visits and meetings are often necessary to find the right property. In contrast, Other Sales Profiles may not require as much research and planning.

6. **Trust:**

   In Real estate sales, personal trust between the agent and buyer is critical. Buyers are looking for someone who they feel they can trust with their significant investment. In contrast, in other sales profiles, trust is often placed in the organization or brand.

7. **Multidimensional knowledge:**

   Real estate sales requires agents to have multidimensional knowledge, including knowledge of international and local market trends, budget and ROI considerations, and intra-stromal developments. In contrast, Other Sales Profiles may require less specialized knowledge.

8. **Sales cycle:**

   Real estate sales typically involves a longer sales cycle than Other Sales Profiles, with multiple processes involved in between, such as property inspections, negotiations, and loan processing.

9. **Personalized attention:**

   In Real Estate Sales, personalized attention is critical at every step of the process, including property selection, loan processing, and registration. In contrast, Other Sales Profiles may require less personalized attention to each customer.

Of course, it's important to remember that a career in real estate sales also comes with its own set of challenges, such as irregular income, high competition, and stress due to high-pressure sales and tight deadlines. It's also important to keep in mind that the nature of the real estate industry can vary greatly depending on location, so it's important to do research on the real estate market in the area where you plan to work.

I am sure you will feel excited, and you will want to start it right now. At the same time, you must be apprised of common myths which may lead to frustration.

Chapter 3

Who Should Choose a Real Estate Sales Career?

Real estate sales can be a lucrative and fulfilling career choice for individuals who are self-motivated and driven to succeed, those who are interested in a career that allows for a potentially high income and the ability to be their own boss, and those who are looking for a career that doesn't require a significant upfront investment.

Real estate sales can be a good fit for those who enjoy working with people, have strong communication skills, and are comfortable with a certain level of uncertainty and risk. Additionally, individuals who are interested in the housing market and are passionate about helping people find their dream homes may find a real estate sales career highly fulfilling.

a. **Don't want to invest a lot of money to start a business,** then real estate sales may be the perfect fit for you. The start-up costs in this career are minimal, and you can work as a real estate salesperson or broker on a commission basis, avoiding the need for significant upfront investment.

b. **Don't want to take bigger risks,** then real estate sales may provide a low-risk option as you can learn on the job, grow your network, and build a steady stream of income over time.

c. **Even if you don't have higher education,** you can still pursue a successful career in real estate sales. This field values experience, work ethic, and practical skills over formal education.

d. **If you have big dreams,** real estate sales can be an excellent platform for you to achieve your financial and personal goals. With hard work, determination, and the right mindset, you can achieve financial stability and success under the right mentor or guidance.

e. **Ready to learn and develop new skills everyday;** real estate sales is a dynamic field that requires ongoing learning and development. You'll need to stay up-to-date on market trends, local real estate laws and regulations, and sales techniques to succeed.

f. **Want to retire early?** Real estate sales can provide the potential for early retirement as the income earned in this field is often big and can fetch you 20 years of income in just 10 years,

Overall, real estate sales can be a fulfilling and lucrative career choice for individuals who are seeking a flexible and low-risk business opportunity.

Chapter 4

The Myths About a Career in Real Estate Sales

Here are a few of the most common myths I have encountered, who came to me to start their career in Real Estate.

a. **Real estate sales is not a respectful profession:** This myth is false. Real Estate Sales requires strong communication, negotiation, and organizational skills and can be a rewarding and well-respected career for those who work hard and are dedicated to providing excellent service to their clients. Providing excellent after-sales services can help establish a deeper connection between a business and its customers. When a business goes above and beyond to ensure that its customers are satisfied and taken care of, it can create a sense of loyalty and trust that can last for years. By being attentive and responsive to the needs of customers after a sale, a business can develop a personal relationship with them, almost like a family friend.

b. **This is a get-rich-quick scheme:** The notion that a real estate sale is a "get-rich-quick" scheme is a false myth. While it is true that the field offers the potential for high earnings, building a successful career in real estate requires time, hard work, dedication, and patience. Just like any other profession, success is not achieved overnight. It is important to remember that the path to success is a journey, and the process of building a thriving real estate career requires consistent effort, continuous learning, and a long-term approach. As the saying goes, "slow and steady wins the race," and this sentiment is echoed in the famous song, "Hum Honge Kamyab Ek Din."

c. **This is an unorganized sector:** This myth is also false. The Real Estate industry is a regulated sector with strict laws and regulations, and many successful real estate companies have established processes and systems in place to ensure a high level of professionalism and organization. The Real Estate (Regulation and Development) Act, 2016, commonly known as RERA, was introduced to bring about greater transparency and accountability in the Indian real estate sector. Prior to the introduction of RERA, the real estate sector in India was largely unregulated, and many builders and developers were operating in an unorganized and non-transparent manner. This lack of regulation resulted in many problems for home buyers, including project delays, construction defects, and the misappropriation of funds.

Since its introduction, RERA has played a crucial role in organizing the real estate sector by establishing a comprehensive regulatory framework. The act has created a system of checks and balances that has increased transparency, accountability, and professionalism within the industry. Builders and developers are now required to register their projects with the regulatory authority, and they are also required to adhere to strict guidelines related to construction quality, project timelines, and fund utilization.

One of the most significant benefits of RERA has been the establishment of trust between home buyers and builders. RERA has empowered home buyers by giving them the tools they need to make informed decisions about their investments. The act has also established a mechanism for dispute resolution, which has resulted in many favorable verdicts for home buyers.

Overall, RERA has played a critical role in transforming the real estate sector in India. The act has created a more organized, transparent, and accountable industry, which has benefited both home buyers and builders. By establishing trust and confidence in the sector, RERA has helped to drive growth and development in the real estate market, which has had a positive impact on the economy as a whole.

d. **A real estate career is easy and requires little work:** Some people may believe that a career in real estate sales is easy and requires little work, but the opposite is true. Being a successful real estate salesperson requires a significant amount of effort and hard work. People need to be knowledgeable about the local real estate market, knowledgeable about the local communities and stay current on industry trends and best practices.

It's worth noting that the real estate industry is dynamic, and the requirements, regulations and best practices are constantly changing. It is important to gather knowledge and educate oneself on the current market and industry standards.

Why People Fail in Real Estate Sales Careers

In the early days of my real estate career, I used to attribute my lack of earnings to the market and those around me. However, as I gained more knowledge and closely observed the reasons why people fail, I discovered the following factors.

1. **Lack of preparation:** Some people may enter the field of real estate sales without fully understanding the industry, the regulations or the local market, leading to failure in attracting clients or closing deals.

2. **Insufficient marketing and lead generation:** Many people fail to generate enough leads to sustain their business; without an effective marketing strategy and lead generation, it can be difficult to find and convert potential clients.

3. **Poor communication and negotiation skills:** Real estate sales require effective communication and negotiation skills. Agents who lack these abilities may struggle to close deals, build client relationships and represent their clients well.

4. **Lack of persistence and perseverance:** A career in real estate sales can be challenging, with many obstacles to overcome. Agents who are not

persistent and do not persevere through difficult times may not be successful in the long term.

5. **Not adapting to changing market conditions:** The real estate market is constantly changing, and agents & brokers who do not stay informed and adapt to these changes may struggle to stay competitive and find success in the industry. While it's difficult to pinpoint specific Indian brokerage companies that failed solely due to not adapting to changing market conditions, there have been instances where companies have struggled and even closed down due to a combination of factors, including failure to adapt to changing market conditions. Here are a few examples:

    a. **Zoom Estate:** Zoom Estate was an online brokerage platform that aimed to disrupt the traditional real estate brokerage model in India by offering a technology-driven, transparent, and cost-effective solution for property transactions. However, the company failed to gain traction in the market and eventually shut down in 2018, **citing a lack of funding and market acceptance as the main reasons.**

b. **HDFC Realty:** HDFC Realty was the real estate brokerage arm of HDFC, one of India's largest financial institutions. The company offered advisory, transactional, and property management services to clients across the residential, commercial, and retail segments. However, the company faced challenges in the wake of the government's demonetization policy in 2016, which led to a slowdown in the real estate market. In 2018, HDFC Realty announced that it was shutting down its brokerage business due to lack of profitability.

These examples illustrate the importance of adapting to changing market conditions in the real estate industry and how failure to do so can have significant consequences for businesses, regardless of their size or market position.

Not understanding the importance of customer service

A career in real estate sales relies heavily on building strong relationships with clients, and providing excellent customer service is crucial for success. **Agents who neglect this aspect of their business may not be able to retain clients or generate repeat business.**

Not following the legal and ethical requirements

Real estate industry is heavily regulated, and not following laws, and regulations can lead to significant legal and financial consequences, as well as damage to one's reputation in the industry.

Additionally, in my team of 200 & more people, I have observed further reasons for success and failure. While many are highly successful, there are some who have not been able to succeed.

a. **Weak mindset:** People may know that certain habits or behaviors are not conducive to success, but they continue to engage in those habits anyway. For example, a real estate salesperson may know that smoking is detrimental to their health, but they continue to smoke. A weak mindset can be a major roadblock to success in real estate sales. For example, an agent may have a limiting belief that they are not capable of achieving their goals, or they may not fully believe in their ability to succeed in this field. This lack of confidence can affect their motivation, drive, and overall performance, leading to failure.

b. **Casual attitude:** A casual attitude towards their work can be a significant contributing factor to failure in real estate sales. For example, an agent may not put in the necessary effort and time to research the market, stay up-to-date on industry trends, or network with other professionals in the field. A lack of professionalism and dedication can result in missed opportunities and reduced success.

c. **Taking it as a side business or part-time:** Real estate is a highly competitive industry that requires significant time, effort, and commitment to succeed. Unfortunately, many people make the mistake of approaching real estate as a part-time or side business rather than a full-fledged business. This mindset often leads to failure, as these individuals fail to give the industry the level of attention and dedication that it requires.

   In order to succeed in real estate, it is important to recognize that this is not a part-time or side business. Rather, it is a full-fledged business that requires a comprehensive approach to planning, organizing, and execution. Like any other business, success in real estate requires a clear business plan, a well-defined target market, a strong brand identity, effective marketing and sales strategies, and a commitment to ongoing learning and professional development.

One of the main reasons that people fail in real estate is that they do not treat it as a true business. They may not invest the time, money, or resources necessary to build a successful career in the industry. They may also lack the focus and discipline that is required to achieve their goals.

In order to avoid this pitfall, it is important to approach real estate with a business-oriented mindset. This means committing to a full-time schedule, investing in the necessary training and education, developing a comprehensive business plan, and seeking out mentorship and guidance from experienced professionals. By approaching real estate as a true business rather than a part-time or side venture, individuals can increase their chances of success and achieve their financial and professional goals in this dynamic and rewarding industry.

d. **Lack of patience:** Real estate sales can be a slow and steady process, and it can take time to close a deal. Agents who lack patience may become frustrated when they do not see immediate results, and they may give up too easily rather than continue working towards their goals.

e. **Attitude:** A negative attitude can impact the success of a real estate Salesperson in several ways. For example, an agent who is easily discouraged or who has a defeatist mentality may struggle to close deals or build positive relationships with clients. This can result in missed opportunities and reduced success.

f. **Lack of self-discipline:** Self-discipline is crucial for success in real estate sales, as it helps agents stay organized, manage their time effectively, and follow through on their tasks and responsibilities. Agents who lack self-discipline may struggle to meet their goals, and they may miss important deadlines and opportunities.

g. **Cannot work under any supervision:** Some real estate salespersons may struggle to work effectively under supervision, as they may prefer to work independently. However, in real estate sales, it is often necessary to work closely with a team, follow a sales process, and receive feedback from a supervisor. Agents who cannot work under supervision may struggle to achieve success in this field.

h. **Not coming out of comfort zone:** In order to succeed in real estate sales, it is important for agents to be willing to step outside of their comfort zone and try new things. For example, they may need to learn new technologies, network with new clients, or try new sales techniques. Agents who are not willing to take risks and try new things may miss out on opportunities for growth and success in this field.

i. **Fake commitment to the client:** Fake commitments to clients are a major problem in the real estate industry, and it is a common reason why people fail in this profession. Many agents or salespersons make false promises to clients in order to make a sale and earn a commission. For instance, they may promise high returns on investment, even when the property in question is not likely to appreciate in value or generate significant rental income.

   In some cases, agents may even try to sell legally questionable properties just to earn a commission. They may not hesitate to put their client's money into the wrong property simply because they are motivated by their own profits. This can result in a loss of trust and credibility and ultimately lead to failure in the industry.

Moreover, when clients realize that they have been misled or given false information, they may take legal action against the agent or brokerage, which can be a major blow to their reputation and financial stability.

In the long run, agents who make fake commitments to clients are likely to have a difficult time building a successful career in real estate. It is essential for agents to prioritize honesty and transparency in all their dealings with clients and to always act in their clients' best interests. This is the only way to build a solid reputation and establish trust with clients, which is crucial for long-term success in the industry.

j. **Not able to handle short-term success:** One of the major reasons why some agents and salespersons fail in the real estate industry is that they are not able to handle short-term success. This can often happen when someone is new to the industry and experiences a sudden influx of money or a few successful deals. While this initial success can be very exciting, it can also lead to complacency and a lack of motivation to continue working hard.

In some cases, agents and salespersons who experience short-term success may begin to take their clients for granted. They may start to prioritize their personal time over their work, spending more time with family, going out to parties, watching movies, and engaging in other non-work-related activities during work-hours. This can lead to a decline in their work ethic and a lack of focus on their client's needs and interests.

This situation can be especially problematic because clients can quickly sense when they are being neglected or treated as secondary priorities. They may become frustrated with the lack of attention and may choose to work with other agents or salespersons who are more dedicated and attentive to their needs.

It's important for agents and salespersons to maintain a long-term perspective and to view their success in the real estate industry as an ongoing process rather than a short-term goal. They should be committed to providing the best possible service to their clients and working hard to maintain their trust and loyalty.

To avoid falling into the trap of complacency and overconfidence, agents and salespersons should set clear goals for themselves and strive to constantly improve their skills and knowledge. This can include staying up-to-date on market trends and changes, networking with other professionals in the industry, and seeking out new opportunities to expand their business.

In the end, agents and salespersons who are able to handle short-term success and maintain a long-term perspective are more likely to build successful and sustainable careers in real estate sales.

It is important to keep in mind that a successful career in real estate sales requires a combination of market knowledge, industry expertise, strong business acumen, and a willingness to continuously learn and adapt to changing market conditions

Chapter 5

The Success Mantra And Its Components

> *"The mantra for being successful in real estate sales is to continually improve and focus on providing excellent customer service."*
>
> **~Sachin Arora**

Here are a few key elements that can help real estate agents or salespersons put this mantra into action and achieve success:

Knowledge: Stay informed and up-to-date on market trends, regulations, and industry's best practices. Continuously educate yourself to stay ahead of the competition. Real estate sales is more than just selling properties. It involves providing a wealth of knowledge to clients on the real estate market, loans, locations, and much more. Real estate salespersons must have in-depth knowledge of the real estate market to provide clients with the best possible advice. They need to stay up-to-date on market trends, including the most recent sales data, the current supply and demand, and the latest industry news.

Networking: Build and maintain strong relationships with clients, colleagues, and industry professionals. Attend events and join professional organizations to expand your network and find new opportunities.

Marketing: Develop and implement effective marketing strategies to reach potential clients and showcase your properties. Utilize technology, social media, and other marketing channels to build your brand and promote your listings.

Customer service: Always put the needs of your clients first and provide excellent customer service. Build trust and rapport with your clients by being responsive, transparent, and proactive in addressing their needs and concerns.

Adaptability: Be flexible and open to change. Stay up-to-date with the latest technologies and trends, and be willing to adapt to changes in the market and in your client's needs.

Discipline: Manage your time and resources effectively and stay organized. Set goals, prioritize tasks, and be consistent in your work habits to achieve success in real estate sales.

"Discipline is an essential aspect of my life. I wake up at 6 am every day and make sure to hit the gym, follow a clean diet, and avoid any activities that may put my health at risk. I believe that to achieve success, it is crucial to have a high-performance body and mind, and this can only be attained through consistent discipline and hard work."

Positive attitude: Maintain a positive, optimistic outlook and a can-do attitude. Believe in yourself, your abilities, and your potential for success in real estate sales.

The success factors mentioned above are certainly important in real estate sales; however, I would like to share my personal secret to success that has helped me and others on my team achieve great results.

1. **Self-discipline:** Cultivate a strong sense of self-discipline and hold yourself accountable for your goals and tasks. Stay focused and driven, even in the face of challenges and setbacks.

2. **Time management:** Manage your time effectively by prioritizing tasks, setting deadlines, and minimizing distractions. This will allow you to be more productive and make the most of your day.

3. **Dedication:** Show a high level of dedication to your work and to your clients. This means working diligently and being available whenever necessary, even if it means forgoing holidays from Friday to Monday, which is the most crucial time for real estate salespeople.

4. **Daily meetings:** Attend daily meetings and actively participate in discussions. This helps keep you on track and ensures that you are consistently improving and learning from others.

5. **The P-100 Formula:** The P-100 formula involves connecting with 100 people in your mobile contacts who know you and could potentially buy property from you. Building strong relationships and expanding your network are essential in real estate sales.

6. **Daily learning:** Make daily learning a priority. Read books, attend training sessions, and participate in role-plays to continuously improve your skills and knowledge.

7. **Knowledge of the local market:** Gain a thorough understanding of the local market and be able to answer any questions your clients may have about it.

8. **P-20 Formula:** Reach out to 20 people in your contacts who can work with you as associates. Collaborating with others can help expand your reach and increase your chances of success. By applying the principles of the P-20 formula, I was able to successfully bring together a group of individuals to work towards a common goal. This group included my 3 childhood friends, Sahil Arora, Ankit Sahni, and Sachin Khurana, as well as my cousin, Hardik Bagla, my wife's cousin Ritika Kapoor and numerous other friends and relatives.

9. **Daily appointments and calls:** Schedule daily appointments and make calls to potential clients to build your business and maintain relationships.

10. **Sharpening skills:** Continuously improve and sharpen your skills, such as negotiation, closing, role-playing, storytelling, and client relationship building.

11. **Success system:** Follow a success system blindly, guided by experienced people. This will help ensure that you are following best practices and maximizing your chances of success in real estate sales.

I'd like to share a personal moment that I could not have achieved in this lifetime if I had not followed the above mantra. I diligently followed everything that I had mentioned here, which resulted in me being able to purchase my first expensive and dream car - a Mercedes-Benz CLA. I asked my father to sit next to me as I drove the car, and I cannot express the emotion that I saw on his face. It was next level, and our family could not have imagined having such an expensive car in their lifetime. The feeling was truly unforgettable, and it's something that every son would love to experience. This was all possible because of my hard work and dedication to my profession.

In conclusion, the key to success in real estate sales lies in having a strong work ethic, being dedicated, and continuously learning and improving. By following a success system, developing strong relationships, and honing your skills, you can achieve great results in this challenging and rewarding industry. Remember to stay disciplined, manage your time effectively, and always prioritize the needs of your clients. With these elements in place, you can reach new heights in real estate sales and enjoy a successful and fulfilling career.

"My favorite quote, '*Na sounga na sone dunga*,' has been a guiding principle for my team, leading to great success." At the end of the book, you will find some amazing success stories out of the many that I have helped craft.

You, too, can write your own success story in real estate.

In the following chapters, I reveal every possible step and strategy that can aid you in accomplishing your goals.

Chapter 6

7 Steps to Getting Started in Real Estate Sales

From my experience, I have established certain steps that, if followed, will enable you to quickly start a career in real estate sales.

When I started in real estate, it was so unorganized that it took me 12 years to understand the success pathways.

I don't want you to take such a long time to succeed.

With all that I have shared and am sharing in the following chapters, you will be able to bypass all the mistakes that people typically make and shorten your road and time to success.

You need to go through these steps carefully in order to launch your career.

Here are details for each step of getting started in a real estate sales career:

1. **Check your mental readiness for real estate sales:** This step involves assessing your own mindset and motivation for entering the real estate sales industry. Are you ready for the challenges and hard work that come with building a successful career in real estate sales? Do you have the drive and determination to succeed, even when faced with setbacks and obstacles? Answering these questions honestly will help you determine if you are mentally ready to embark on this new career path.

   In my case, I was one of those people who felt called to pursue a career in real estate sales, despite the risks and uncertainties involved. While many of my friends and peers were taking the safe route and pursuing traditional career paths, I knew my passion for real estate sales was too strong to ignore.

   From the very beginning, I made the decision to establish myself in the real estate industry and to make it my Plan A, rather than settling for a backup plan or a less fulfilling career. I knew that success in this field would require hard work, dedication, and a willingness to take risks and adapt to changing market conditions. But I was willing to take on those challenges in pursuit of my long-term goals.

2. **Enroll your family and friends:** Once you have decided that you are mentally ready for real estate sales, it's important to enlist the support of your loved ones. This includes informing your family and friends of your decision and seeking their support and encouragement as you embark on this new journey. Having a supportive network will help you stay motivated and focused as you work to build your career in real estate sales.

   I can share from personal experience how the enrollment and the support of my family have helped me greatly in my profession. Every weekend, I celebrated sales with my extended family, who functioned as my team. My father served as an accountability partner, asking my team and me about our results and questioning our performance, which helped us achieve our goals faster. He also took on my household responsibilities, allowing me to focus on my business. I can attest that if you can enroll your loved ones, it can work wonders for your career.

3. **Assess your financial situation:** Before starting a new career in real estate sales, it's important to assess your financial situation to determine if you have the resources you need to get started. This may involve reviewing your current income, expenses, and savings

and determining what steps you need to take to ensure that you have a solid financial foundation for your new career. If you are starting out as an agent, you should have enough savings to cover your living expenses for at least 6 to 8 months without any income. On the other hand, if you are a salaried salesperson, you should have a backup plan covering at least 45 days in case of unforeseen circumstances.

Since the nature of the real estate industry involves a lot of fieldwork, you will also need to factor in additional expenses such as fuel for your vehicle, mobile bills, and other office expenditures.

It's important to have a clear understanding of your financial needs and to plan accordingly to avoid any financial stress or strain in the early stages of your real estate career.

4. **Essential Tools and Skills for Real Estate Sales:** Starting a career in real estate sales requires more than just people skills and the ability to sell properties. In today's fast-paced, technology-driven world, it is essential to be equipped with the right computing knowledge and tools to stay ahead of the competition and provide the best possible service to your clients.

One of the basic tools you need to have is knowledge of computer software such as Microsoft Excel, Word, and PowerPoint. These programs are commonly used in real estate to create and analyze spreadsheets, contracts, and presentations. You will also need to be proficient in email communication, as it is the primary mode of communication in the today's era.

Another important tool you will need is a basic understanding of mathematics for calculating property prices, commissions, and other financial aspects of the job. This will help you ensure that all financial transactions are accurate and avoid any mistakes that could result in legal issues.

In terms of hardware, you will need a reliable laptop, smartphone, or tablet to stay connected with clients and colleagues on the go. Additionally, having a two-wheeler or other mode of transportation can be essential for traveling to property viewings and client meetings.

By investing in the right computer knowledge and tools, you can position yourself as a knowledgeable and efficient real estate salesperson and stand out in a competitive market. These skills and tools will not only help you to increase your productivity but also provide better customer service to your clients.

5. **Decide the model:** When starting a career in real estate sales, you should consider the following models:

    a. **Independent Real Estate Agent:** In this model, you work as an independent contractor and are responsible for all aspects of your business, including lead generation, marketing, and administrative tasks.

    b. **Broker's Team:** In this model, you work as part of a team of agents who are affiliated with a broker. You have access to the broker's resources, including leads, training, and marketing materials, but you may have to share a portion of your commission earnings with the broker.

    c. **Franchise Model:** In this model, you work as an sub-agent for a established real estate service provider (agent). You have access to the resources and support provided by the franchisor, but you may have to pay a fee or share a portion of your commission earnings with the franchisor.

    These are the three most common models in real estate sales, and the best choice will depend on your individual goals, skills, and preferences. It's important to consider the pros and cons of each model and weigh the trade-offs carefully before making a decision.

Here's a comparison of the three models of real estate sales:

Independent Real Estate Agent

- **Pros:** Complete control over your business, keep all commission earnings, freedom to set your own schedule
- **Cons:** Responsibility for all aspects of business, including lead generation and marketing, investment of time and money in building your brand and reputation.

Broker's Team

- **Pros:** Access to a network of resources and support, including leads, training, and marketing materials, benefit from the broker's established reputation and brand.
- **Cons:** Sharing a portion of your commission earnings with the broker, less control over business decisions, following established guidelines and procedures set by the broker.

Franchise Model

- Pros: Access to resources and support provided by the franchisor, benefit from the established brand and reputation of the franchise.

- **Cons:** Paying a fee or sharing a portion of your commission earnings with the franchise, following established guidelines and procedures set by the franchisor.

Again, the best model for you will depend on your individual goals, skills, and preferences. It's important to consider the pros and cons of each model and weigh the trade-offs carefully before making a decision.

My recommendation

If you don't have any experience and you don't want to risk your money & time, I would recommend starting with a Broker's Team in your location.

Choosing a Brokers Team: If you decide to join a broker's team, the next step is to choose the right broker for you. This involves researching different brokers and teams and comparing their services, fees, salaries and commission structures. Look for a broker that aligns with your goals and values and who has a proven track record of success in the real estate sales industry.

When choosing a broker to join their team, it's important to consider the following factors:

a. **Reputation:** Look for a broker with a solid reputation in the industry, one who is well-respected by clients, colleagues, and other professionals in the real estate community.

b. **Experience:** Consider the level of experience the broker has in the real estate industry, as well as their track record of success.

c. **Support and Training:** Look for a broker who offers a comprehensive support system, lead and sales closure support, including training and resources to help you succeed in your real estate career.

d. **Commission Structure:** Understand the broker's commission structure and how it will affect your earnings. Make sure it aligns with your financial goals.

e. **Work Culture:** Look for a broker who has a positive, supportive culture that aligns with your values and goals.

f. **Technology and Tools:** Consider the broker's technology and tools, including their customer relationship management system, marketing materials, and technology infrastructure.

g. **Location:** Choose a broker who is based in a location that aligns with your target market and where you plan to focus your business efforts.

By considering these factors and doing your due diligence, you can choose a broker who will be a strong partner in your real estate career and help you, to achieve your professional and financial goals.

6. **Set aside time for learning and practicing:** Building a successful career in real estate sales requires a strong foundation of knowledge and skills. That's why it's important to set aside time each day for learning and practicing the script. This may involve reading industry-related books, attending training sessions and workshops, and practicing your pitch and negotiation skills.

7. **Take massive action every day:** The final step to building a successful career in real estate sales is to take massive action every day. This means putting in the time and effort to learn and grow as a salesperson and actively pursuing new clients and opportunities. The more action you take, the more you'll grow your skills and your business, and the closer you'll come to achieving your goals. Most people get confused as to what massive action they need to take every day. Here are the core actions which helped my team to achieve success.

Network: Attend local real estate events and join industry organizations to meet other real estate professionals and expand your network.

Connect with other agents and brokers, as well as potential clients, through social media and in-person events.

Consider participating in mentorship programs or finding a seasoned agent to act as a mentor and guide you in your early career.

Build your brand: Develop a professional image, business card, and email signature. Create an internet profile to showcase your listings and promote your services.

Establish a strong presence on the internet, such as LinkedIn, Facebook, and Instagram. Differentiate yourself from other agents by developing a unique selling proposition (USP) that highlights your strengths and expertise.

Market yourself: Advertise your services to potential clients through a variety of channels, including email, direct mail, and web-world. Reach out to past clients and ask for referrals to expand your network. Participate in open houses and other events to promote your listings and meet potential clients. Consider offering home buyer or seller seminars to educate the public and establish yourself as a knowledgeable and trustworthy agent.

Stay current: Continuously educate yourself on industry trends, regulations, and best practices through continuing education courses, industry conferences, and professional development opportunities.

Stay informed about local real estate market conditions and changes in property values and tax laws. Utilize technology and digital tools to streamline processes and provide a better experience for your clients.

Focus on building relationships: Building trust and rapport with clients is key to success in real estate sales.

Listen to their needs, be responsive and accessible, and work tirelessly to meet their goals. Provide excellent customer service, follow up regularly, and be a reliable and knowledgeable resource for your clients throughout the buying or selling process.

Stay organized: Maintain accurate and up-to-date records of your clients, properties, and transactions. Utilize a CRM (customer relationship management) system to track leads, communications, and appointments.

Create a system for following up with clients and keeping them informed throughout the buying or selling process.

Develop negotiation skills: Study negotiation tactics and techniques to become an effective negotiator on behalf of your clients.

Learn to communicate clearly and assertively while also being empathetic and understanding of the other party's perspective.

Practice your negotiation skills through role-playing and real-life transactions.

Build a referral network: Provide excellent service to your clients, and ask for referrals from satisfied customers.

Develop relationships with other professionals in the real estate industry, such as mortgage lenders, inspectors, and contractors, to create a referral network.

Consider offering incentives or bonuses to clients who refer business to you.

Stay motivated: Set achievable goals and regularly track your progress to stay motivated and on track. Celebrate your successes and learn from your mistakes.

Surround yourself with positive and supportive people, and consider joining a real estate coaching or accountability group. Staying motivated is a key aspect of success in any career, including real estate sales. One way to stay motivated is to surround yourself with positive and supportive people who can provide encouragement and support when things get tough.

As the analogy goes, just as coal turns red due to the fire and its surroundings, you, too, can experience a positive transformation by surrounding yourself with the right people. This may include other successful real estate agents, supportive family members, friends, and mentors who can offer guidance.

Chapter 7

7 Guiding Principles for a Successful Real Estate Sales Career

Real Estate Sales is a rewarding and challenging career that has the potential to bring great financial rewards and professional satisfaction. To be successful, you must understand the fundamentals of the business, have the right attitude, and have a firm set of guiding principles. In this section, we will look at 7 guiding principles that can help you achieve success in your Real Estate Sales career. I am living these principles every day without fail. Thanks to the people around me who taught me these principles.

1. **Understand that success comes from building relationships:** In real estate sales, relationships are the foundation of success. Building strong relationships with clients, teams and other professionals in the industry is essential to being successful. As a real

estate salesperson, you must focus on developing strong connections with customers and colleagues in order to have success. This involves actively networking and making yourself available to others. You should also be open to hearing feedback and be willing to adjust your approach when necessary.

It's important to listen to what your clients need and want. Ask questions, be patient and truly understand their needs. Showing that you genuinely care about them can make all the difference. Being friendly and professional, yet personable and knowledgeable, is essential for building relationships. Also, always follow up after meetings or phone calls and make sure to stay in touch with your contacts.

By creating and nurturing strong relationships with your clients, you can better understand their needs and help them make informed decisions about their real estate investments. Developing strong relationships with other professionals in the industry is equally important. These connections will help you stay informed about the latest trends in the market and build a solid reputation as a reliable real estate agent.

In addition to acknowledging the importance of clients, I attribute a significant portion of my success to the strong relationships I have built with my team. I recognize that investing in my team's development and well-being is essential to achieving our shared goals. By prioritizing the growth and satisfaction of my team members, they are more likely to be engaged, motivated, and productive, ultimately contributing to a positive and successful work environment.

The key to my success lies in the way I treat my team. Right from the beginning, I have made a conscious effort to build a familial atmosphere among us. I value each and every member of my team, and I make it a point to remember important details about them, such as their personal milestones like EMI payments, birthdays, insurance coverage, and their children's school schedules. This level of attention to detail and care for their personal lives has helped me to earn the trust and respect of my direct reports and their subordinates and has contributed to our overall success as a team.

2. **Don't be afraid to ask for help:** As a real estate salesperson, there is no shame in asking for help. If you are struggling to make progress or unsure of how to proceed with a certain client, reach out to more experienced colleagues or mentors in the industry

who can provide advice and guidance. Asking for help is not a sign of weakness - it's a sign of wisdom. You may find that experienced agents have invaluable tips and tricks that can help you be successful.

It's also important to remember that there is a vast support network available to you. From online forums and webinars to industry-specific courses, there are many ways to get the knowledge and resources you need. Don't be afraid to explore these options when you feel overwhelmed or lost.

Being a successful real estate salesperson is all about managing time wisely, taking risks, and making smart decisions. But at the end of the day, it's also about being able to ask for help and being open to advice from experienced professionals in the field. Don't be afraid to lean on others for guidance. Doing so can be a powerful tool for success!

3. **Believe in yourself:** Having self-confidence is essential in any profession, especially in the real estate sales industry. It's important to trust your own judgment and have faith in your abilities. Believing in yourself gives you the strength and courage to handle challenging situations, as well as the drive to strive for success.

One way to build self-confidence is to take time to recognize and celebrate your accomplishments. Keep track of what you do right, and use this knowledge to reinforce your sense of worth. Remember that even small victories are worthy of acknowledgement.

Another way to believe in yourself is to focus on the positive. Think about how far you've come and how much you have achieved. Dwelling on past mistakes and failures will only erode your self-confidence. Acknowledge these moments, learn from them, and then move on.

Finally, cultivate an attitude of gratitude. Be thankful for all that you have, from the skills and experiences that have gotten you to where you are today to the opportunities that lie ahead. When you practice gratitude and appreciate all that life has to offer, it is easier to believe in yourself and your abilities.

4. **Stay focused and organized:** Being successful in a real estate sales career requires staying focused and organized. A key part of this is having a clear vision of what you want to accomplish and then creating a plan to get there. This can involve breaking down goals into manageable pieces and creating a timeline for when each goal should be accomplished. Additionally, it is important to have a system in place

for managing leads and tracking progress. This can be done through various software programs or even an old-fashioned spreadsheet.

Organization also extends to daily tasks such as keeping up with paperwork and responding to emails or calls in a timely manner. Additionally, staying organized can help you avoid distractions that may take away from your productivity. Make sure to keep a close eye on your priorities and stick to your schedule.

Finally, don't forget to take time for yourself. Being organized and staying focused doesn't mean you have to constantly be working. Take breaks throughout the day, and make sure you get plenty of rest. This will help ensure that you are recharged and ready to tackle all of your responsibilities the next day.

5. **Be coachable:** Being coachable is one of the most important qualities to have when starting a real estate sales career. Coaches or mentors can offer invaluable advice, guidance and support in navigating the challenging and often overwhelming world of real estate. It is essential that you are open to learning from those around you and taking constructive feedback on board.

Your real estate coach may be able to give you insight into different markets, share strategies for success and provide tips on how to stay focused and organized. They may also help you set goals and provide encouragement when you're feeling overwhelmed or frustrated. Be sure to express your appreciation for their help and stay open to trying new things.

It is important to remember that being coachable does not mean blindly following instructions. You need to be willing to experiment, take risks, and challenge ideas. Ask questions and trust your instincts when making decisions. Don't be afraid to speak up if something doesn't feel right. The best coaches understand that their job is to provide you with the tools you need to make successful decisions, but ultimately the decisions will be yours to make.

6. **Persevere:** One of the most important principles for success in any career, including real estate sales, is to persevere. No matter how difficult it may seem, you must never give up. Challenges and setbacks are inevitable in any industry, and you have to have the resilience to keep going. Even if you make mistakes or experience rejections, don't let that discourage you. Instead, take it as a learning opportunity and use it to improve yourself and your skills.

When faced with challenging times, stay positive and remember why you started this career in the first place. Reflect on the successes that you have had and the goals that you want to achieve. Don't forget to ask for help when needed, but ultimately, remain resilient and never give up. With hard work, dedication and perseverance, you can reach your goals and be successful in your real estate sales career.

As I sit down to pen this book today, I am reminded of a poignant incident from my life. It was the day my second son, Bunny, was born, and my wife had been admitted to the hospital. As a dutiful husband and father, I was expected to be by their side at all times. However, due to a property exhibition being organized by my team, my presence was required there. So I had to switch between both places.

Despite the difficult circumstances, I made it a point to ensure that neither my work nor my family felt neglected, even though it meant being away from my newborn child and wife. I knew that this temporary sacrifice would pave the way for a better and financially stable future for my entire family in the long run. And as it turned out, my decision paid off.

7. **Give back:** One of the most important principles for a successful real estate sales career is to give back to your community. Giving back doesn't have to be a monetary donation, although that would be an added bonus. You can give back by volunteering your time or services, such as offering free seminars or workshops in your area.

You can also give back by sharing your knowledge and experiences with others, as I have been doing by grooming and mentoring people on my team and now am doing on a larger scale with this book.

When you're in real estate sales, it's important to foster relationships with people in your community. Giving back to them shows them that you care and appreciate their patronage. It also allows you to develop relationships with potential clients, which can help your business grow. Giving back can also build trust with clients and create a positive reputation for yourself. By giving back, you can make a difference in the lives of those around you while building a successful real estate sales career at the same time.

Giving back to your community is a crucial principle for a prosperous real estate sales career.

Like I said earlier, this book, which contains the strategies and information that I have personally used to achieve success in the field, is an example of giving back.

Similarly, you can also contribute by giving away things such as money, time, or valuable information that can make someone else's life easier and more comfortable.

I have shared with you all the key steps, principles, and strategies that have proven to be successful in my own real estate sales career and those of numerous others.

These principles have enabled me to achieve more than I ever thought possible at such a young age. Today, I am proud to lead a team of over 200 dedicated individuals who are like family to me.

Financially, I have achieved my dreams of owning my dream cars and upgrading my home to a larger and more beautiful space. All of this is thanks to my career in real estate sales.

“If you are born poor, it’s not your mistake, but if you die poor, it’s your mistake”.

~Bill Gates

The Success Stories

Bonus Chapter

As promised, here are a few of the many miraculous success stories people have achieved following the same success mantra and strategies I have revealed in this book. All these people are working with me as my extended family.

Success Story: Jitender Ramdev

Jitender Ramdev's journey in Real Estate with me has been a story of transformation and growth.

Starting as a graduate with a modest salary of 18,000/- per month in a private bank and just a two-wheeler to his name, Jitender is now the proud owner of three properties and two cars.

With a lavish lifestyle, Jitender attributes his success to the 12 years of working with me in real estate sales.

The experience has not only boosted his financial stability but also had a profound impact on his personal life.

In his own words, "Sachin Arora Bhai's guidance and support through Sales Armor have not only improved my financial security but also shaped my life vision and enhanced my overall well-being. The bond between us feels like a family connection, and I am grateful for the positive changes that have come my way."

Success Story: Vikas Tyagi

Vikas Tyagi, with an MBA, transformed his financial situation after joining the Sales Armor Team. **When he started out, he was living in a rented house in Delhi, but now he drives a Range Rover Velar and an Audi A4 and lives in his own flat in Noida. He also owns approximately 5 properties in NCR and rebuilt his hometown home, costing around 1.5 crores. He has been with Sachin Sir in Real Estate for 10 years.**

The benefits he has gained from joining Real Estate Sales include:

1. **Unlimited potential for success within the Sales Armor Team.**
2. **Protection from uncertainty without added cost.**
3. **A family-like bond stronger than blood relations.**
4. **Living and enjoying luxurious lifestyle elements such as cars, homes, brands, and trips**

Success Story: Avinash Srivastava

Before joining my real estate team, Avinash Srivastava was struggling to make ends meet with his PGDM (MBA) degree. He was living paycheck to paycheck and sometimes even had trouble affording food. However, after 10 years and 4 months with the team, Avinash's life has changed dramatically.

He now has assets worth 4 crore rupees and has the confidence and financial stability to achieve anything he sets his mind to.

Working with my team has not only transformed Avinash's financial situation but has also expanded his thinking which has given him a new perspective on life.

He no longer fears taking on new challenges and feels empowered to make his mark in the world. With this support and guidance, Avinash has truly found his path to success.

Success Story: Dharmendra Kumar

Dharmendra Kumar is a successful individual who holds an MBA degree.

When he first started, he had a loan of INR 2 Lakhs and only owned a bike worth INR 35,000.

However, after joining the real estate industry, he invested in two plots in Agra and gradually upgraded his vehicles, starting from an i10, then a new i10, an XUV 500 in 2018, and finally, a top model of Tata Harrier.

Over the course of 11 years of working in the real estate industry, **he has benefited greatly from the professional relationship.**

In his words, "Sachin Sir is not just a boss but a mentor and a guardian. He provides a family-like culture and always acts as an elder brother in times of both happiness and difficulty. His priority is for all of his employees to earn well and live comfortably, and he takes great joy in their successes. Furthermore, Sachin values transparency and honesty in his dealings, with a heart that is always willing to support his team."

Success Story: Yogesh Mishra

Yogesh Mishra holds an MBA and started his career with a first salary of 5000. Before joining me, his average income is 300000/month. He has been associated with me for 9 years.

Yogesh's life has undergone a transformation since he joined my team.

He has received three promotions in a year and acquired valuable assets, such as a Fortuner car, a plot of land, and more wealth, enabling him to live a good lifestyle.

This is what Yogesh has to say," I credit all of this to Sachin sir's guidance and leadership, who treats his team members as family and takes care of their needs. Yogesh's life goal is to retire alongside Sachin Sir, and he doesn't see any other option. I even follow Sachin sir's example and have been celebrating my birthday, my son's birthday, and my anniversary by feeding underprivileged slum/beggar children at good restaurants for the past four years.

Success Story: Deendayal Arya

Deendayal Arya, who holds a B.Com, M.Com, and PGDBA, has previous work experience of 9 years. Before joining the real estate industry, he struggled to make ends meet and had no savings to fall back on.

However, after a decade of working in real estate alongside me, Deendayal has undergone significant personal growth and development.

He has acquired valuable skills in self-discipline, time management, team management, and people skills, among others, which have contributed to his overall personality development.

As a result of his hard work and success in the real estate industry, **Deendayal now owns three properties and has gone on more than 10 international trips. He also drives a top-of-the-line automatic SUV car (his third vehicle) and has moved his family from a slum area to a golf-centric property in Noida.**

Success Story: Ravi Hinduja

Education: B.com

Previous experience before joining me: 8 years

Financial situation before starting in real estate: Rs 50k/month

Before joining Real Estate, Ravi was struggling with his finances and lacked discipline in his life. He worked in a different industry but was not satisfied with his work environment and growth opportunities.

However, after 8 years of joining the real estate sales team, Ravi experienced a drastic change in his life.

With guidance and training, he developed strong self-discipline and time management skills, leading to financial freedom.

Ravi's hard work and dedication paid off as he upgraded from walking to now driving a Mercedes. He honed his leadership skills and saw unexpected growth in all aspects of his life, including his personal and professional development.

Ravi became a part of a supportive and energetic team that works together, learns together, and enjoys each other's success.

He also developed a new thought process and gained a deeper understanding of the power of writing and manifestation.

Ravi's overall experience with the real estate sales team and working culture were unlike anything he had experienced in his 14 years of working experience.

Success Story: Kalam Khan

Kalam Khan, a postgraduate with a stable financial background, **has seen a significant improvement in his financial situation after joining the Real Estate industry.**

He has been in this field for 6 years and has benefited greatly from his association.

The disciplined working culture has helped Kalam develop a strong work ethic, and the financial hunger that never dies has driven him to strive for more. **He has gained the courage to take bold decisions and is always on the lookout for new markets and opportunities to grow.**

Additionally, Kalam has learned to see big dreams **and has been instrumental in creating new leaders in the industry.**

Success Story: Chirag Kapoor

Chirag is a member of our Sales Armor team.

Chirag joined our team back in 2014 after a few false starts in the sales industry. He had been working in a small sales company with 40-50 people, where he was earning only Rs. 6,800 per month.

After just 6 months, he left that job and tried his hand at a BPO, where he earned Rs. 11,000 per month. However, he only stayed in that job for 6 months before his sister (my wife) and I approached him with an opportunity in the real estate industry.

Finally, Chirag Kapoor decided to join our team in February 2014. From that point on, he never looked back.

Within a year of joining our team, he purchased his first family car, a Hyundai i10.

Within 6-7 months of working with us, he was earning in lakhs, which was a game-changer for him at the age of 19-20. His hard work and dedication paid off even more when he purchased a brand-new Jeep Compass in 2018.

In 2019, Chirag achieved a major milestone by purchasing a commercial property. This was a testament to his hard work, as well as the support and guidance that he received from our team.

Chirag's success story is a testament to the power of having the right team and support system in place.

I am extremely proud of Chirag and the progress he has made in his career, and I am confident that he will continue to achieve great things in the future.

Success Story: Prateek Kapoor

Prateek was a B.Com graduate who, prior to joining the real estate industry, was a fresher with average academic performance. Driven by a desire to achieve financial independence at an early stage in life, he searched for a well-paying and fulfilling job.

Six years after joining me in the real estate sector, Prateek has seen a remarkable transformation in himself, with **notable improvements in his overall personality development.** He has developed **critical skills such as self-discipline, time management, team management, and other important interpersonal skills,** which have made him more efficient and effective in his work.

From having nothing in hand to now owning several residential and commercial properties, Prateek has been able to achieve financial freedom and strong resilience.

At the young age of 25, he has even been able to purchase a luxury car and lead a fulfilled life.

Success Story: Shauzab Kazmi

Shauzab Kazmi, an MBA with a good family background, **joined the Real Estate industry to meet his goals and personal desires.**

He has been in this field for 5 years and has benefited greatly from his association.

The disciplined working culture has helped him to develop a strong work ethic, and the best mentorship allowed him to obtain financial freedom without taking any help from his family. **Within these five years, he out-performed many and became the Gurugram branch head for my team, 'Sales Armour'.**

Additionally, today he owns many properties and drives a luxury SUV after his BMW and has learned to lead under pressure and also trained 30 leaders for this team under my supervision.

Success Story: Azhar Mirza

Education: BA in Economics

Previous experience before joining my team: 12 years

Financial situation before starting in real estate: Rs 0

Before joining real estate

- Azhar was struggling with his finances and lacked discipline in his life.
- He was doing business with his father and then worked with different real estate companies but was not satisfied with his work environment and growth opportunities.

After 4 years of joining real estate

- Azhar experienced a drastic change in his life after joining the real estate sales team with me.
- With Sachin's guidance and training, Azhar developed strong self-discipline and time management skills, leading to his financial freedom.
- Azhar's hard work and dedication paid off as he upgraded from walking to now driving a BMW 5 SERIES.

Success Story: Rohit Singh

Name: Rohit Singh,

Education: MBA

Previous experience before joining my team: 12 Years

Financial situation before starting in Real Estate on my team: Rs 00

Before Joining Real Estate

- Rohit was struggling with his finances and lacked discipline in his life.
- He was working in a different industry and was unsatisfied with his work environment and growth opportunities.

After 2 years of Joining my Real Estate Team

- Rohit experienced a drastic change in his life after joining the real estate sales team.
- With Sachin's guidance and training, Rohit developed strong self-discipline and time management skills, leading to his financial freedom.

- Rohit's hard work and dedication paid off as he upgraded from walking to now driving a Mercedes.
- He honed his leadership skills and saw unexpected growth in all aspects of his life, including his personal and professional development.
- Rohit became a part of a supportive and energetic team that works together, learns together, and enjoys each other's success.
- He also developed a new thought process and gained a deeper understanding of the power of writing and manifestation.
- Rohit's overall experience with the real estate sales team and working culture were unlike anything he had experienced in his 14 years of working experience.

Success Story: Anmol Bhatia

Anmol belonged to a small town and had no knowledge about the real estate industry.

After completing his B.Com in his hometown, he decided to shift to Noida under my guidance.

After 9 years of Joining real estate and my team:

- **Anmol achieved his target of shifting his family to the metro city and providing them with a better life.**
- **He also achieved his dream of owning his own house, building good wealth, and buying his dream car.**
- Anmol has seen unexpected growth in all aspects of his life, including his personal and professional development.

He could not imagine achieving all this at such a young age.

There exist several remarkable success stories, such as Garvit, who purchased a Range Rover at the young age of 26, Sharda, who bought a BMW X1 soon after owning an i10, Nakul, who has been driving a Fortuner since his fifth year of employment, Manish Tyagi (Monu), who acquired a BMW X5 at the age of 29, Aman, who possesses both a house and an Audi-A6 before turning 27, Hardik, who obtained a Mercedes C class right before his marriage at the age of 28, and Adhiraj, who not only owns a luxurious vehicle but a collection of high-end cars. Furthermore, Rupal, born in 1996, purchased a Fortuner Legender at an early age. These are only a few of many similar stories that could be recounted another time. However, I earnestly aspire to document your own story in a similar vein.

As you read through these success stories, it's natural to wonder how you can reach the same level of achievement or even surpass it.

You need not wonder any longer!

The wait is indeed over.

With All That I Have Shared
In This Book, You Could Be
The Next Success Story!

Author's Note

If you are planning to start a career in the real estate industry, it is essential to equip yourself with the right techniques and strategies that can help you succeed in this highly competitive field.

One way to gain this knowledge is by referring to books and other educational resources that offer valuable insights into the real estate sales process.

This book that you have in your hands is a comprehensive guide to help you understand the ins and outs of the real estate industry and to develop the skills and knowledge you need to excel in this field.

It covers all the key aspects of real estate sales, including lead generation, client management, property marketing, negotiation, and closing deals.

However, reading this book alone may not be enough to guarantee success in your real estate career. **It is essential to practice what you have learned and implement these techniques in real-life situations.**

All that I have achieved is by implementing whatever I learned. Currently, I live with my two kids, Shaurya and little one to who I call "Bunny", my doting wife, and my mother. Setting and meeting new goals and dreams daily by Enjoying next level of challenges in my own way playing with them, while having a two seater in my car collection along with owning my dream villa and adding.

Of course, we still face problems like everyone else, but as we climb the ladder of success, the level of problems we encounter also tends to increase. **However, we have learned to handle difficult situations wisely and efficiently.**

I am not suggesting that problems are exclusive to certain individuals or that some people are immune to them. **Challenges are an inevitable part of life for everyone, regardless of social status or profession.**

The key lies in how you approach and manage these difficulties.

With a strong and resilient mindset, one can navigate through tough times with relative ease.

So whenever you are faced with challenges, reach out for help.

You can seek out mentorship and guidance from experienced real estate professionals, attend seminars and workshops, and continue to educate yourself on the latest trends and best practices in the industry.

I am committed to providing guidance and support to those starting out in this exciting and challenging field.

Best of luck in your real estate career!

Best Wishes

~Sachin Arora

Stay Connected:

sachin_arora17

sachin.arora.3538039

sachinaroralc

sachin-arora-598333139

realtywithsachinarora.com

@salesarmour2.0

www.ingramcontent.com/pod-product-compliance
Lightning Source LLC
LaVergne TN
LVHW010112170826
845678LV00012B/2372